A is for Anointed

The Alpha and Omega for who you are in Christ

by
Gretchen Harris

Illustrated by
david munoz

For my beautiful daughters, Kristian Nicole and Selah Marie. May you grow to know who you are in Christ.

A is for Anointed @ 2017 All Rights Reserved
GRETCHEN HARRIS

A

I am the apple of His eye. Keep me as the apple of your eye; hide me in the shadow of your wings.

I am the body. But in fact God has placed the parts in the body, every one of them, just as he wanted them to be.

B

C

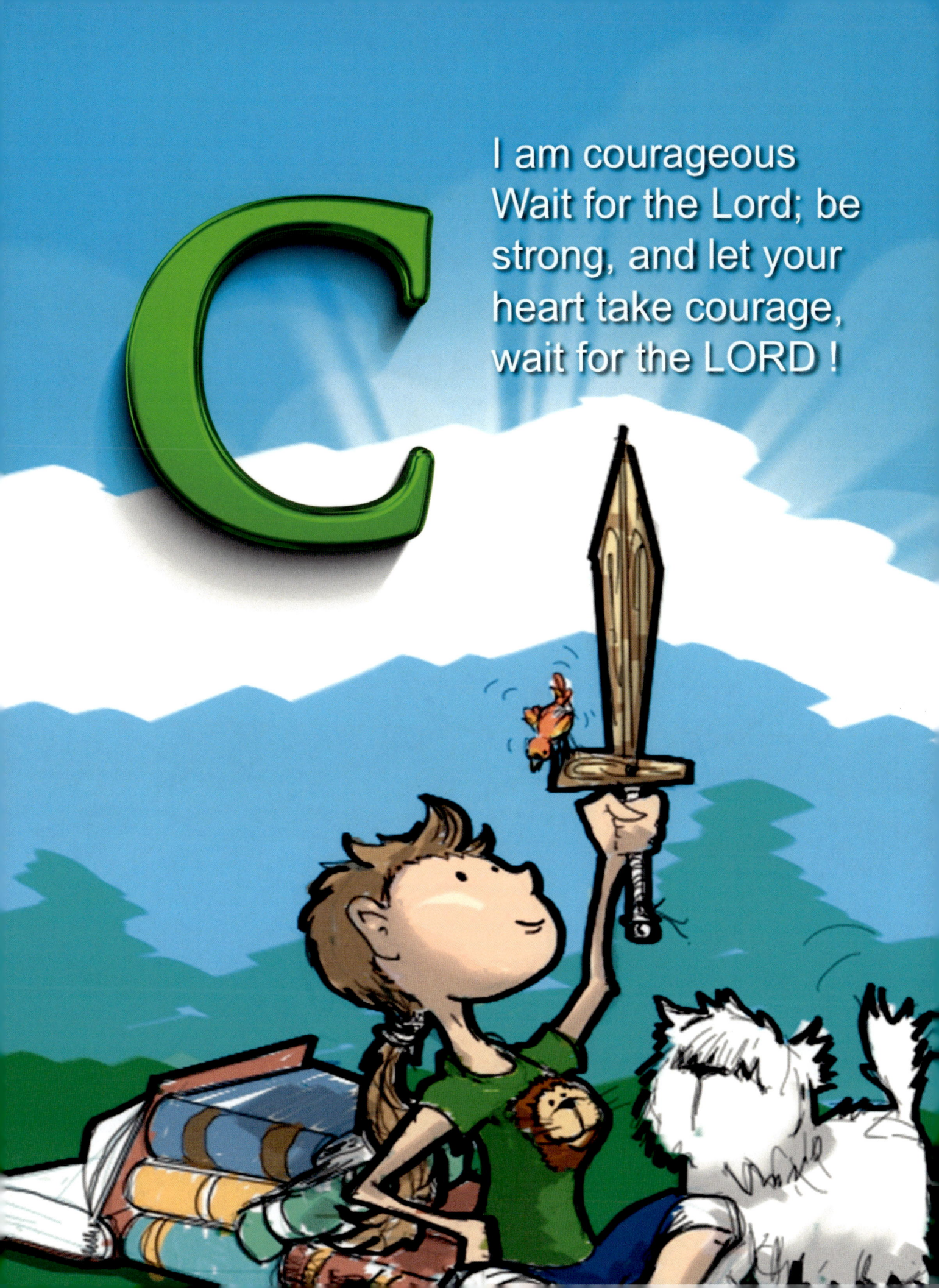

I am courageous
Wait for the Lord; be strong, and let your heart take courage, wait for the LORD!

I am a disciple.
"If you abide in my word, you are truly my disciples, and you will know the truth, and the truth will set you free ".

E

I am an eternal spirit. I give them eternal life, and they shall never perish; no one will snatch them out of my hand.

F

I am favored. For those who find me find life and receive favor from the Lord.

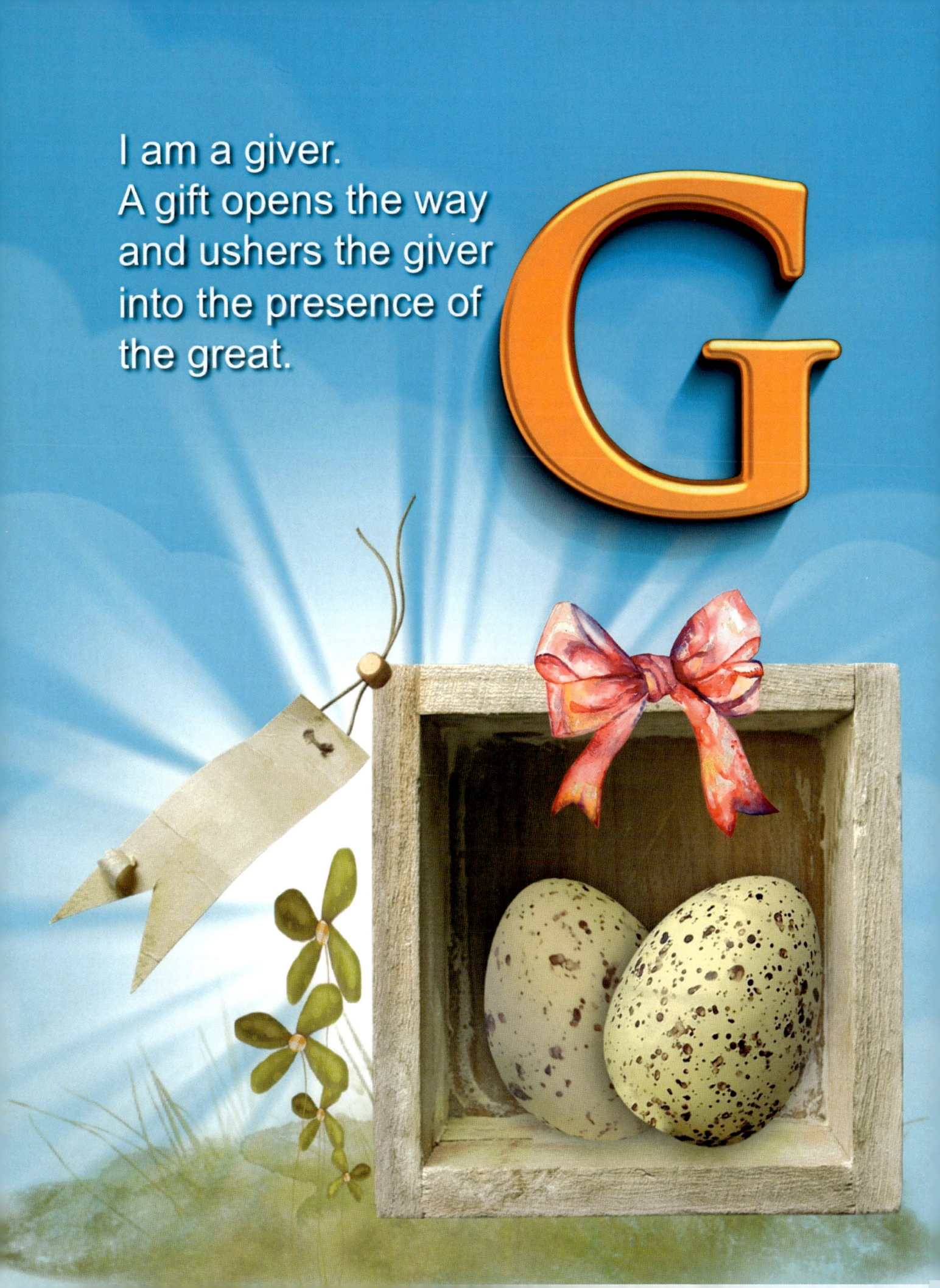

I am a giver.
A gift opens the way
and ushers the giver
into the presence of
the great.

G

H

I am the HEAD and not the tail.
The Lord will make you the head, not the tail....you will always be at the top, never at the bottom.

I

I am made in His image. So God created mankind in his own image, in the image of God he created them; male and female he created them.

J

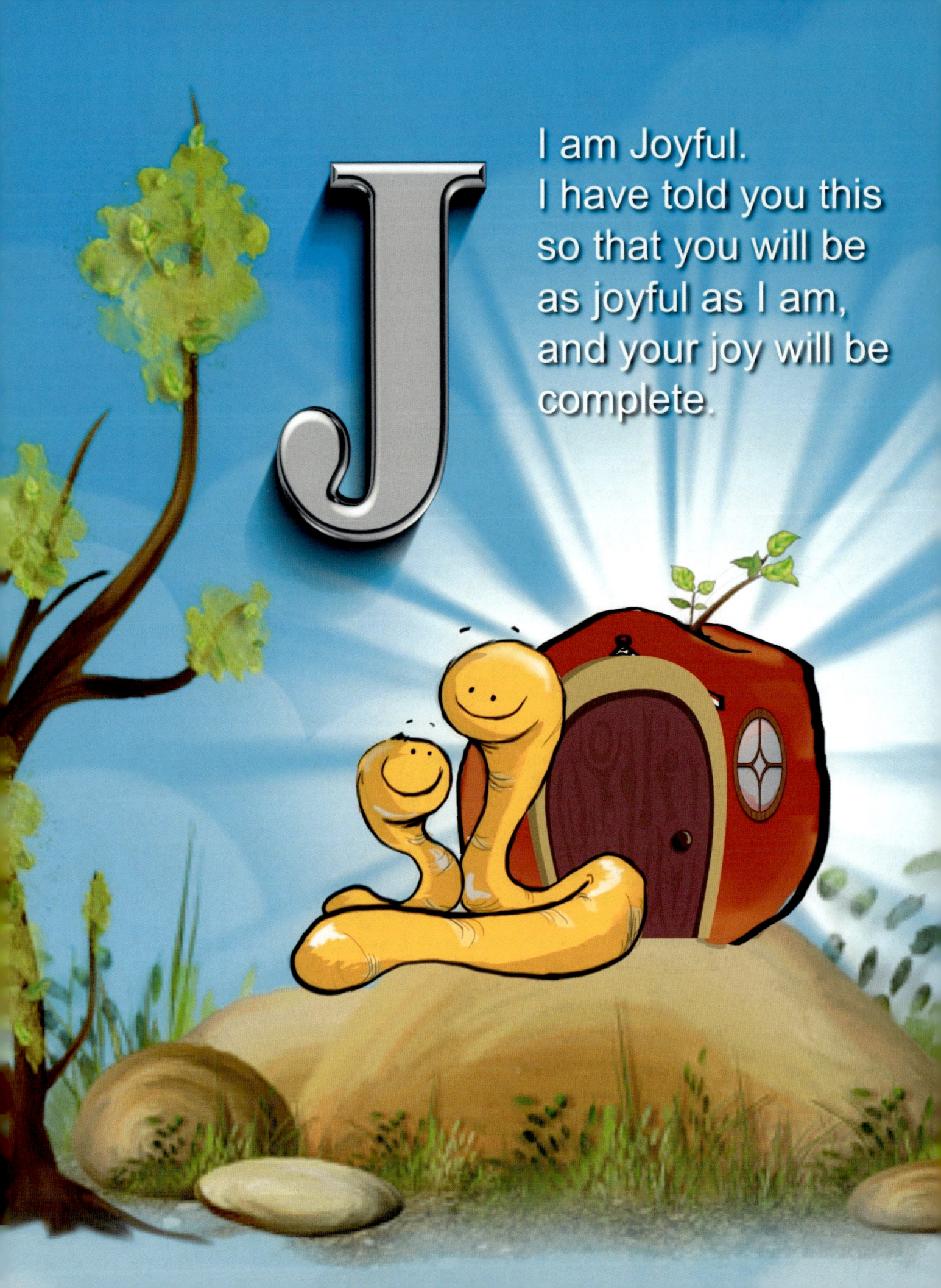

I am Joyful.
I have told you this so that you will be as joyful as I am, and your joy will be complete.

K

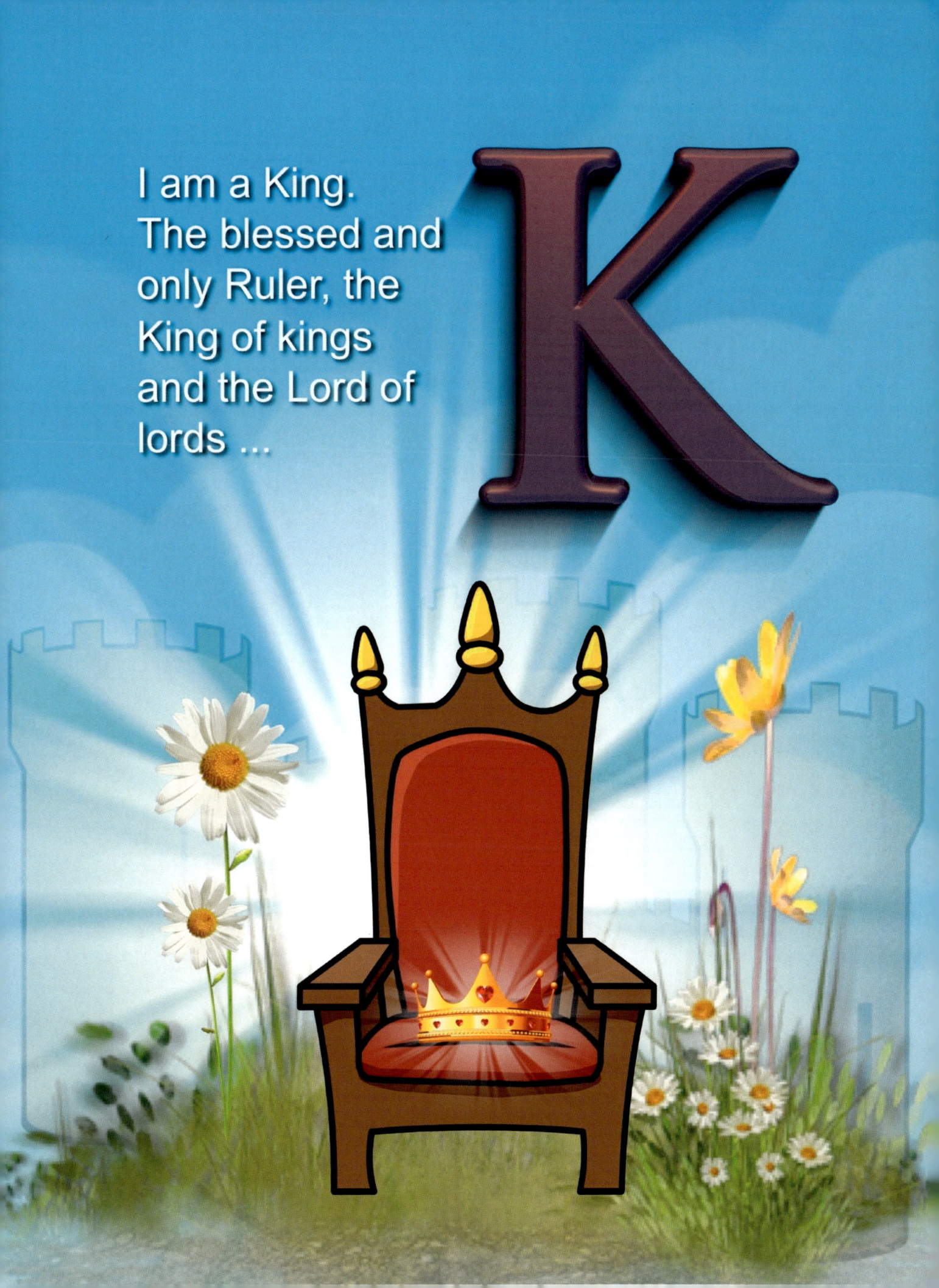

I am a King. The blessed and only Ruler, the King of kings and the Lord of lords ...

L

I am loved. For God so loved the world that he gave his one and only son, that whosoever believes in him shall not perish but have eternal life.

M

I am fearfully and wonderfully made. I praise you because I am fearfully and wonderfully made; your works are wonderful I know that full well.

N

I am a New creation. Therefore, if anyone is in Christ, the new creation has come: The old has gone, the new is here!

I am an Overcomer.
For everyone born of God overcomes the world.

O

P

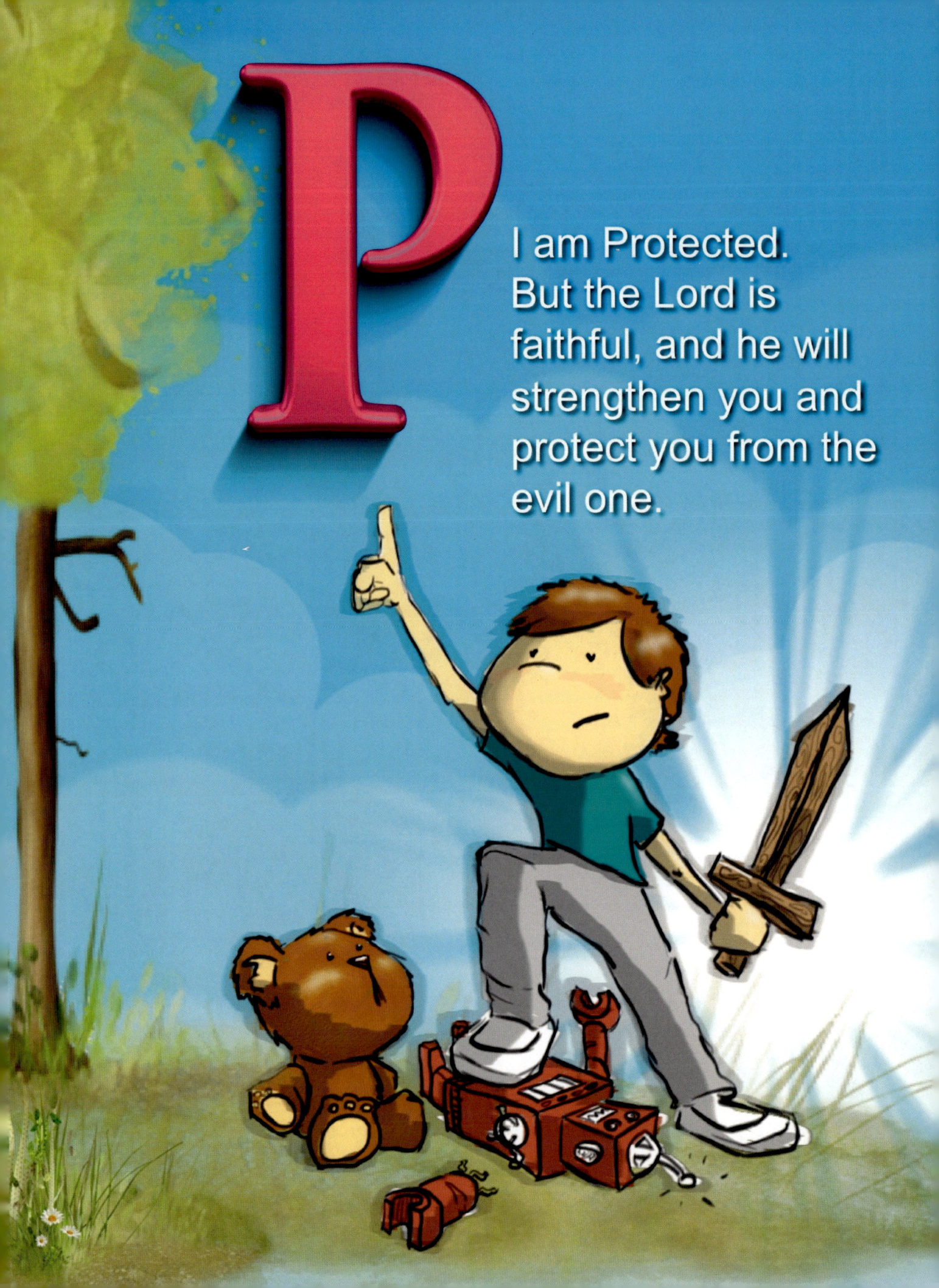

I am Protected. But the Lord is faithful, and he will strengthen you and protect you from the evil one.

I am Qualified.
It is not that we think we are qualified to do anything on our own.
Our qualifications come from God.

R

I am Redeemed. Christ redeemed us from the curse of the law by becoming a curse for us.

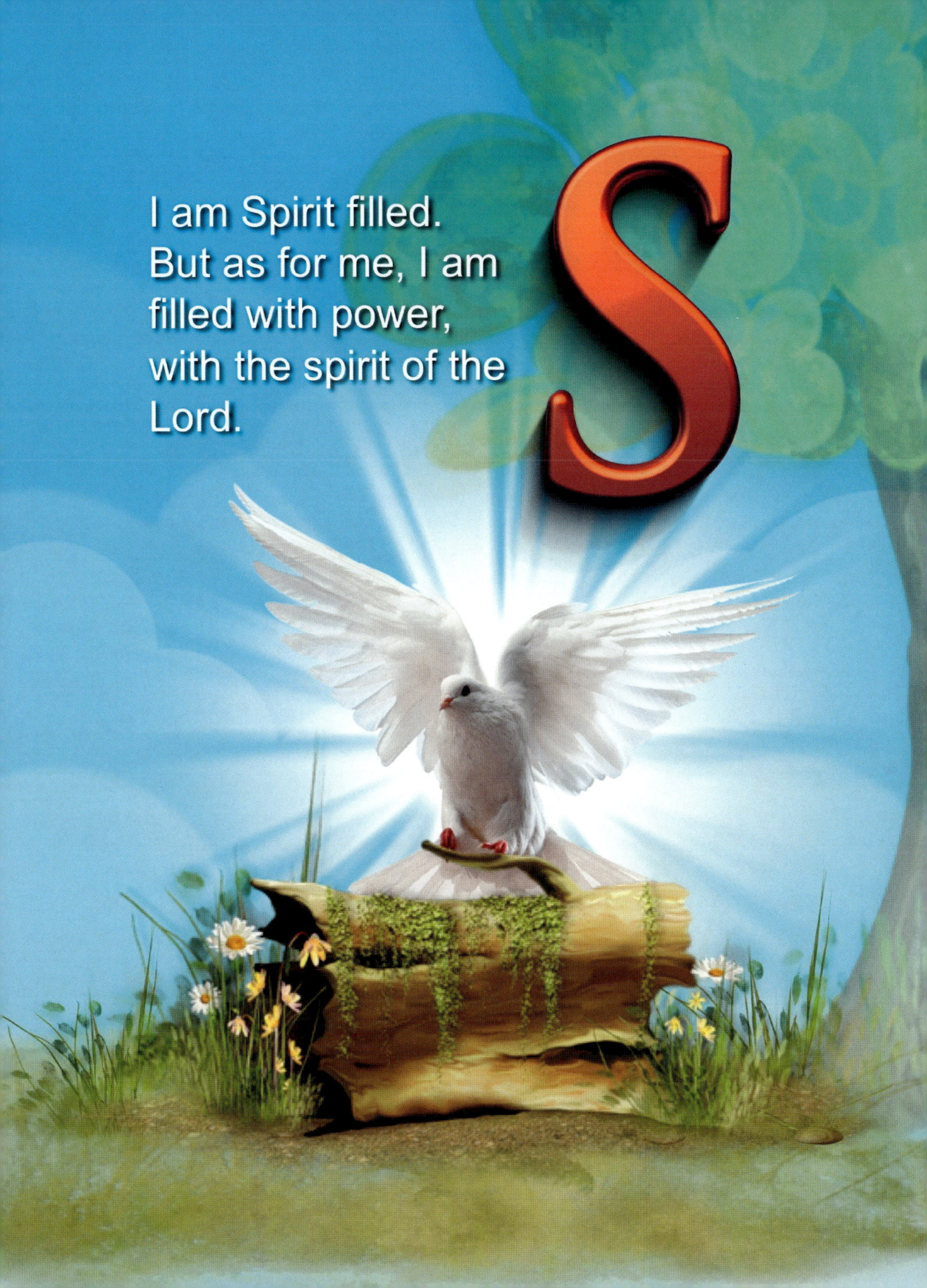

I am Spirit filled. But as for me, I am filled with power, with the spirit of the Lord.

S

T

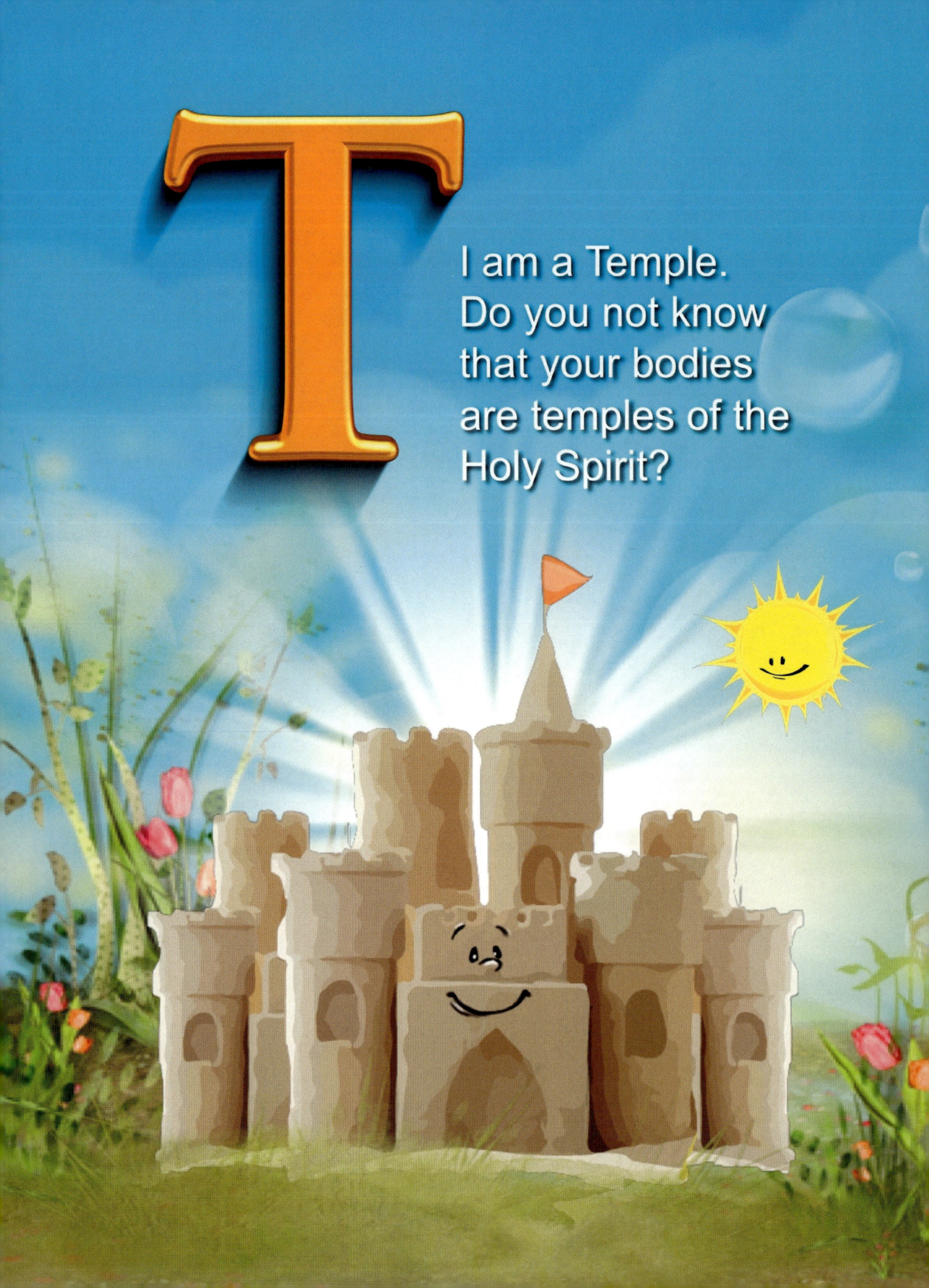

I am a Temple. Do you not know that your bodies are temples of the Holy Spirit?

U

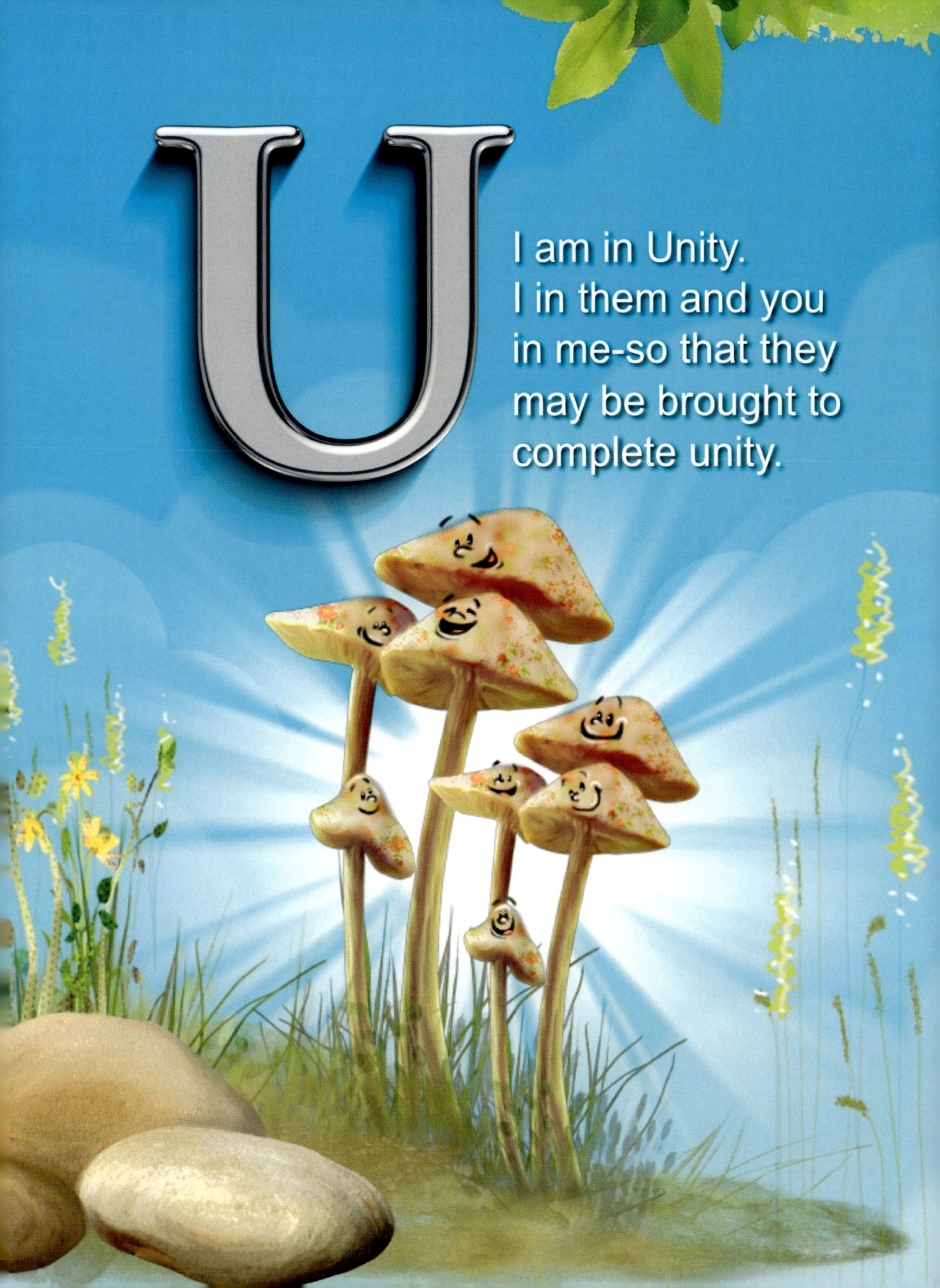

I am in Unity. I in them and you in me-so that they may be brought to complete unity.

I am Victorious. For the Lord your God is the one who goes with you to fight for you against your enemies to give you victory.

V

W

I am a Warrior. The Lord is a warrior; the Lord is his name.

X

I am a spirit of eXcellence. Whatever your hand finds to do, verily, do it with all your might.

Y

I am Yielded. Neither yield your members as instruments of unrighteousness unto sin: but yield yourselves unto God.

Z

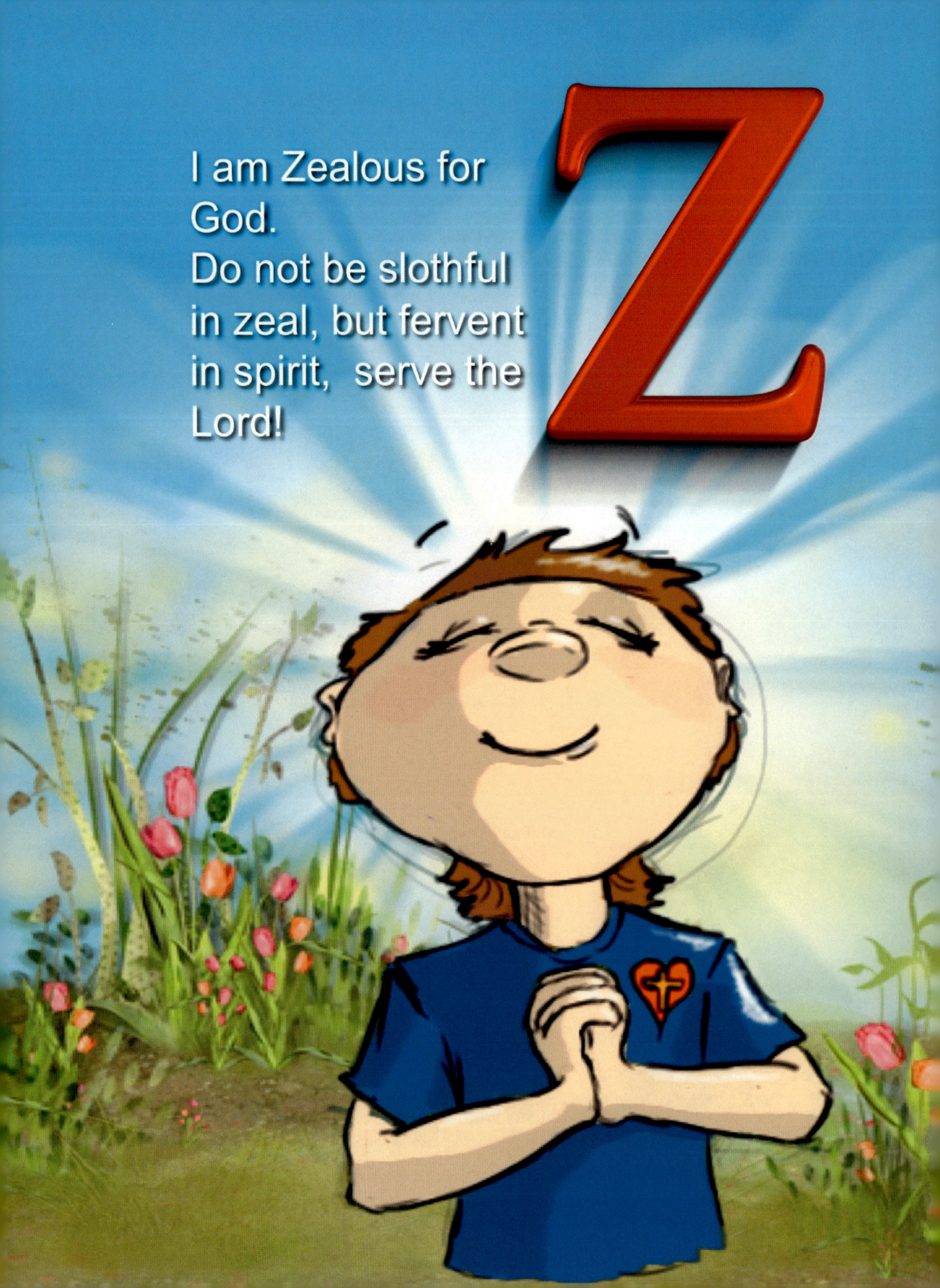

I am Zealous for God.
Do not be slothful in zeal, but fervent in spirit, serve the Lord!

THE END

A is for Anointed @ 2017 All Rights Reserved
GRETCHEN HARRIS

Scripture References

Letter A Psalm 17:8
Letter B 1 Corinthians 12:18
Letter C Psalm 27:14
Letter D John 8:31-32
Letter E John 10: 28-30
Letter F Proverbs 8:35
Letter G Proverbs 18:16
Letter H Deuteronomy 28:13
Letter I Genesis 1:27
Letter J John 15:11
Letter K 1 Timothy 6:15
Letter L John 3:16
Letter M Psalm 139:14
Letter N 2 Corinthians 5:17
Letter O 1 John 5:4
Letter P 2 Thessalonians 3:3
Letter Q 2 Corinthians 3:5
Letter R Galatians 3:13
Letter S Micah 3:8
Letter T 1 Corinthians 6:19
Letter U John 17:23
Letter V Deuteronomy 20:4
Letter W Exodus 15:3
Letter X Ecclesiastes 9:10
Letter Y Romans 6:13
Letter Z Romans 12:11

Salvation Prayer

Lord Jesus, thank you for loving me and dying for me on the cross. I declare that your precious blood cleanses me of every sin. I believe you rose from the grave and that you are alive today. I receive you as my Lord and Savior, now and forever. I am now a beloved child of God and heaven is my home.

Beloved Readers,

As a parent, teacher, and believer it is my heart's desire to breathe the living word of God in to the life of every child who encounters this book. May you learn to see yourself as God sees you. The scripture references show that this book was inspired by God and his word will not return void. This book is not a work of fiction, but a reflection of who God says you are. May this book be a blessing to your family for generations to come.

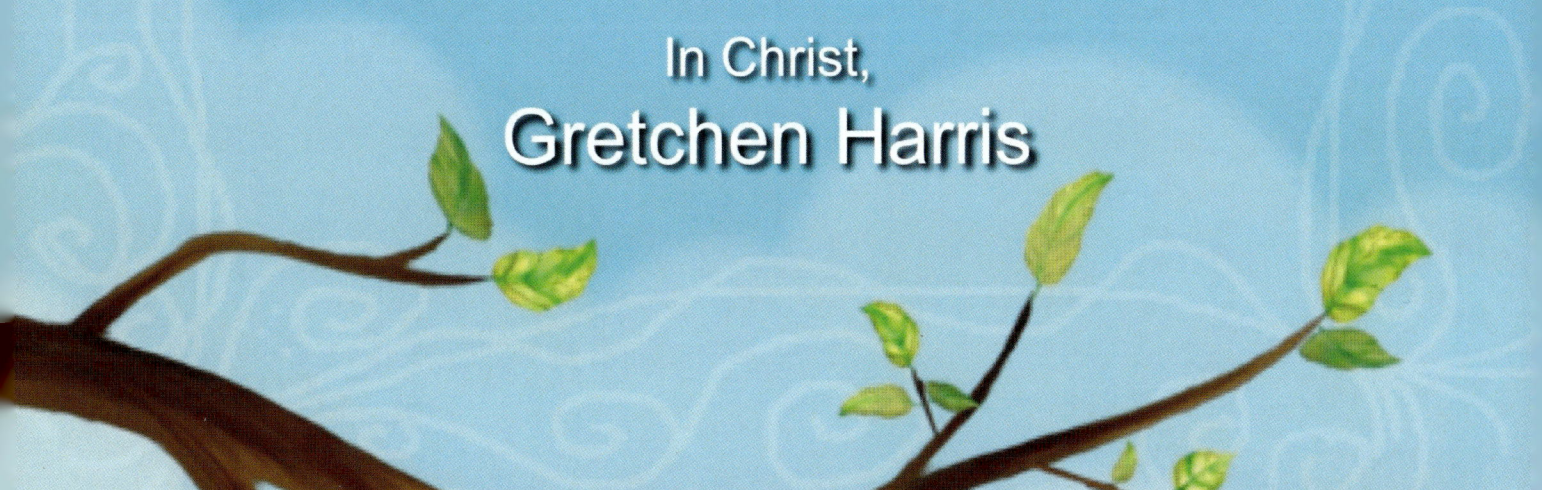

In Christ,
Gretchen Harris

Manufactured by Amazon.ca
Bolton, ON